Road Trip

Barbara Loots

Kelsay Books

Cover photo: B.K. Loots

ISBN 13: 978-0615989037

Kelsay Books
White Violet Press
24600 Mountain Avenue 35
Hemet, California 92544

For Gail White—mentor, pen pal, poet extraordinaire

Acknowledgments

Blue Unicorn "Gardens" "Degas: The Morning Bath"
Cedar Rock "The Waterfall" "The Source"
The Christian Century "The Penitent Magdalene"
The Formalist "Summer Sapphics at St. Simon's Island"
The Helicon Nine Reader "Advice to a Younger Woman"
I-70 Review "At Blackwater Lake"
Landscapes With Women "Refrigerator Poem" "Conversation"
      "Touring the Capitol" "On the Beach at the Strait of Juan
      de Fuca"
Light "Eviction"
The Lyric "Theology" "Small Things" "Barcarolle Chinoise"
      "What Did You Do in the War, Daddy?" "When I Become
      Transparent" "Separations"
Measure "The Boat Builder"
Mezzo Cammin "Road Trip" "Down the Road from Graceland"
      "Sisters" "New Year's Eve" "At the Gate"
Missouri Poets: An Anthology "Lovers After a Long Time"
The Muse Strikes Back "Aubade on Troost Avenue"
Negative Capability "Seashore Sestina"
New Letters "Handling the Evidence" "Squaw Creek"
The Oregonian "When I Become Transparent"
Plains Poetry Journal "Conversation" "Of Mums and Mummies"
      "The State of Absolute Nap" "Still Life With Life"
Poets at Large, Helicon Nine Editions "Separations" "Found
      on a Slip of Paper in a Crack in the Wall"
The Random House Treasury of Light Verse "Hippopotamus"
South Coast Poetry Journal "At the Home"
Voices: Poems from the Missouri Heartland "Devil's Pool at
      Big Cedar Cove"
The Whirlybird Anthology of Kansas City Writers "Villanelle for
      the Road"

Contents

Rites of Passage

Walking on Water

About the Author

Sources

Theology

When silence took the shape of sound
and the first light flashed clear,
what had eyes to see it with
                or ears to hear?

How frivolous a bird's song is,
superfluous the sun--
the unutterable whimsy
                of a dark unknown.

Conversation

After the last, late crying of the birds,
the murmur of a deep rain folds us in.
Our conversation leaves no room for words.
Your silent touch becomes a sound within.

Softly at first, a pulse of ancient drums
sending a message through my wilderness,
while to my hearth the storyteller comes,
the virgin dancer, and the sorceress

strumming their runes of ecstasy and grief
on every nerve like an electric song
till I become the very mouth of life,
wild with the ululation of God's tongue.

Summer Sapphics at St. Simon's Island

Heavy breathing, liquid July in Georgia
fills our lungs with languorous, marshy perfume.
Drugged, we lie on pallets of woven plastic,
broiling our brains out.

Breezes lick the sweat from our thighs and salty
foreheads. Is it skin or the surf that sizzles
so? And who will know when this work of sun is
done to perfection?

Time no longer measured in ticks or pulses
slows to cook us well in our foolish pleasure,
food for hungry gods we have taught to relish
flesh on the seashore.

At Blackwater Lake

Early afternoon and the wind goes softer.
Only poplar leaves have a way to whisper.
Somewhere waves are lapping against a rowboat,
thumping a rhythm.

Hear it? Here's the poem you think you came for,
speaking artless syllables. Never mind your
inspiration. Something is making music
better than you are.

Song goes deep at Blackwater Lake. The burr of
insects eating into the fallen pine trees,
sparrows, bumblebees in the tangled bushes
back of the cottage.

You can hear the hummingbird long before she
swerves in view, a thrumming of small propellers.
Listen. Listen. This is the earth's own poem
perfect and wordless.

Devil's Pool at Big Cedar Cove

Before the lake came up and drowned the spring,
the chill artesian bubbled from below
in every season like a gift, to bring
life back from what had perished long ago.
Before the world was as the world became,
and no one knew that anything was here,
the spring that had no bottom and no name
watered the juniper and slaked the deer.
Before the pool was flooded, natives say,
white, eyeless fish would float up from the deep
like ghosts from a cold hell where bone chimes play,
and spirits of forgotten fathers sleep.
Sometimes, they say, on a still and dreamless night,
moon on that water sinks, sinks out of sight.

Separations

Relentless rain, that ambient metaphor,
enfolds the afternoon in reverie.
The year unravels like a tapestry
shaken by cold wind through a broken door.
The leaves, like words once whispered in the air,
unfasten from their past, and every tree
becomes an unconnected artery
that stains the ground unstemmed, an open fear.
This season when all patterns come apart,
I learn to live unsheltered and alone,
with hands held over an illusive fire.
I feel the dark vein break into my heart,
urged inward like the root that splits the stone
by the energy of unfulfilled desire.

Small Things

Things have a tendency to lose themselves:
hammer, needle, the necessary spring,
a button, the keys—they disappear like elves,
like roses, wishes, the words for everything.

Dive in. Ransack a drawerful of debris.
Wrestle with irritation, grief, self-doubt.
One earring, that pen, eyesight, dignity:
small things we learn, in time, to do without.

Refrigerator Poem

Today is the day I must open the crisper
where something organic has gone into goo.
Today I must counter the visitor's whisper
There's death in this kitchen. I smell it.
                    Don't you?

Today is the day when my conscience must answer
for loss so expensive, and messy, and sad:
today I must have out the vegetable cancer
of careless indifference to things going bad.

The Boat Builder

He bows over the board to hone the line
from stem to stern along a subtle curve
that instinct and intelligence define.

With equal parts exactitude and nerve,
and love's perfection lofted in his soul,
he coaxes perfect from imperfect tools,

in order to achieve the simple goal:
to sail beyond the reach of any rules
but those of wind and water. Cedar curls

in fragrant piles of flotsam at his feet,
while in his mind, a silken wing unfurls,
all plans fulfilled, all purposes complete.

Gardens

You like to shape the landscape, make things grow
beautifully together. As in this English garden
nurtured by dreams crusaders brought back home
from mystic enclaves east of Jerusalem.
Cedars of Lebanon, jasmine, damask rose,
pomegranates (like handfuls of garnet)
and the first lemons Europe had ever seen.

Lost in a green labyrinth, hedges of yew
higher than our heads,
we call each other's names
over the leaves that hide our lovers' games.
This pattern of paths echoes the marble maze
in a French cathedral floor
where pilgrims used to crawl from prayer to prayer.

I remember the flowering squares at Villandry
where Eleanor of Aquitaine and her court talked
incessantly about love—
l'amour tendre, l'amour tragique,
l'amour volage (fickle), l'amour folie—
planted in symbols (pinwheels, daggers, hearts)
that bloom forever in my memory.

Hand in hand, we stroll this English park
of tidy paths, perennials, herbs, and trees,
loving the light that makes this green life grow.
Later, we taste its fragrance in the dark.

The Source

When first I walked out of the ocean
I took with me currents cold and hot,
and silken hands that slid like summer
over the wide back of the sand. I took
the fringe where fishes dart,
the whales' slow rhythm, struts
of lost ships bringing treasures, and
a singing of the conquests yet to come.
I took the rivers' penetrating flow, the deeps
where none but eyeless, breathless
creatures go, the urgency of huge migrations, life
that comes in countless little deaths I do not know.

Places

On the Beach at the Strait of Juan de Fuca

Rocks live slowly. Human life can happen
fast, too fast for what we call our senses.
Happy to have my ashes take their chances
coming back as rock, I'll start a mountain
spewing hot from underneath an ocean.
Rush of dust and steam to stratospheric
heights, I'll make the very air choleric,
smear the sky with primal self-expression,
then subside to wait for tide and season,
seed and bird and vast subcontinental
grind to move me through the elemental
molecules the universe has chosen,
make the dust I was into a diamond,
or fist of granite resting at Port Townsend.

Rice Cottage at Pawley's Island

For once, a few words cannot draw the scene
as well as, say, a watercolor would.
The late sun crosswise of an afternoon
defines the sleepy drift of solitude
here on a slanted porch where windy ghosts
rock in the chairs. Abandoned, the beach gear—
umbrellas, towels, shoes, deflated rafts—
awaits its lively human engineer.
Napping somewhere? Distinctions scarcely hold
in this happy, haunted cottage by the sea,
between the habits of the young and old,
where time lends credence to eternity,
where autumn light defies the written word
like love, or the variations of a mockingbird.

Seashore Sestina

Quick footed, the terns and sandpipers feeding
in the surf outstep in rhythm the crush
of ocean inching over their feet in green
curls. Chutes of sun burst through the cloud
mosaic as invisible salt
sifts into our hair. Nothing appears urgent

except all at once, the fluttery, urgent
departure of the sandpipers startled at their feeding
by a blundering Labrador with salt-
stiff fur, whose careering paws crush
across the shingle. A passing cloud
draws a patch of azure over the green

sea surface, never so many shades of green
as in September, when often the urgent
winds shift and shove the clouds
a thousand ways an hour. Pelicans feeding
not far offshore wheel and crash-
dive, while we two, up to our necks in salt-

water, watch them skim over our heads. Salt
splashes sting our eyes as we float on the green
swells, listening to the landward crush
of the breakers. We let ourselves go with the urgent
gentle undertow. Sometimes we've seen porpoises feeding
just here on fish that shimmer around us now like cloud.

We bob together in this sea as soft as cloud,
a body fluid, a treasure-store of salt
and nourishment for healing, and for the feeding
of our deep memories. Like a return to the green
ferny springs of life, this swim restores our urgent
connection with an ancient earth. (Too soon the crush

of time will try to kill us again, as we crush
ourselves against calendar and dial.) A cloud
trails darkness eastward. Soon urgent
whiffs in advance of a squall whip up the salt
spray and bring us the distinct green
scent of rain. Then, fresh river feeding

the sea, the delicate crush of rain begins feeding
our pleasure, as though this cloud anticipated our green
evening's sweet urgent touches, on skin still tasting of salt.

Villanelle for the Road

The true way may be found, but at a cost.
The dashboard deity presides and judges.
Recalculating really means *You're lost.*

Is this a bridge that I've already crossed?
I wonder as the snake of traffic nudges
between the tollbooths. What's it going to cost?

I have my doubts, refusing to be bossed
by bland advice a nagging voice begrudges,
recalculating how you got so lost.

This muse would never suit you, Mr. Frost.
Bear left. Turn right. Take ramp. She never fudges.
The road not taken clearly has a cost.

But I'm footloose again, my baggage tossed
behind me. Good-bye, all you drudges!
Recalculating, nothing to be lost,

I roll along the road, a stone unmossed,
a stubborn certainty that never budges,
finding my way regardless of the cost,
recalculating, yes, but never lost.

Road Trip

*Ganesha—the elephant deity—is the destroyer
of vanity, selfishness and pride.*

The geographic magazine explained
how brutally young elephants are trained
to carry tourists on their trundling backs
along domesticated jungle tracks
in Thailand, where the work of clearing trees
once brought great herds of giants to their knees.

Meanwhile, and closer by, a new herd grows
in Wal-Mart parking lots, lined up in rows,
of chrome-tooth beasts exhaling diesel breath
and bringing armadillos certain death
when they roll out on ribbons of concrete
with brutal masters in the driver's seat.

Surrounded by them on the interstate,
I wonder at my lust for other freight,
what unfulfilled ambition like a goad
still prods and pushes me along the road,
while wreckage littering the countryside
shows how Ganesha will be satisfied.

Down the Road from Graceland

Elvis's Death Anniversary
August 16, 1996

Route 78 takes us to the Travelers Rest
near Birmingham. The air-conditioner
has ushered me through dreamland with its whirr
all night. I quarrel with another guest—
a gnat. And then a trucker overhead
awakens, turns the needle shower on.
A trunk lid slams. It's minutes after dawn.
And I remember now:
                                          the King is dead.
Back up the road a-ways in Tupelo,
the fans will gather at the shotgun shack
where he was born to bring his spirit back
in one egregious, sentimental show.

Life is a costume, and you wore it well,
Elvis, when your sequined dream came true
a thousand fold and danced away with you
in blue suede shoes. Those golden records tell
the story of a lonesome boy possessed
by demon music, caught up by the crowd,
and nailed to fame. You made your momma proud
and rich. But still she died.
                                          Well, God knows best,
you might have said. And in the end, you gave
your soul to Graceland, where the pilgrims queue
to view the relics, say a prayer for you,
and pile their plastic roses on your grave.

31

Aubade on Troost Avenue

for Richard Wilbur

The eyes open to a Hopper painting.
It is the Thriftway Cleaners at six in the morning,
hanging for a moment in a hushed gallery
of gray rain. Inside the yellow window
a woman in an orange uniform attends an army

in plastic bags, limp on its hangers,
empty of arms and legs. Back of the counter,
there are the clothes waiting for the daily orders
of fresh feeling, filling whoever will wear them
with the dignity of their crisp dry-cleaning.

Now they are marching in circles as the woman
flips the switch for inspection. Suddenly stopping,
they sway towards her as she slouches to the door,
yawns, stretches, clicks the lock, and turns
the red placard from CLOSED to OPEN,

opening so the world can come in and regain
with barely a word, its clothing and its colors.
Oh, let there be nothing today but cleaning,
nothing but warm vapor and the steamy chemical
smell of linen and wool pleated and creased.

Let them emerge from their rank confinement,
these suits and dresses and coats for the well-to-do.
Let heroes go forth in the latest fashion
of fine attitudes while the sleepy attendant
loads and reloads her machine.

Field Trip

In the museum where little children lean
their noses on the glass, one old machine
could crank up two huge disks to make a spark
that leapt a foot or more across the dark.
We wander through this technologic maze
of science's ingenious displays
and talk about inconsequential things,
aware that a celestial silence rings
its mystery around us as we speak.
It is a way to listen that we seek.

Across what space have you and I the stuff
to make a spark? Is death or life enough?
The dancing images of earth and fire
and air and water—all that we aspire
to translate from our incandescent dreams
enters our blood from tributary streams
older than language. Every troubled tongue
teaches its ancient vision to the young,
and we are caught a moment by surprise
to see the lightning in each other's eyes.

In the Museum

Of Mums and Mummies

In the 1800s, tons of mummies were shipped from Egypt
to England, where they were pulverized and used to
fertilize gardens
    —Curator's Note in the Field Museum, Chicago

Let us exhume our relatives at once,
wasted in concrete vaults and crates of steel.
Put the bloom back in the garden with their bones,
and let the rubbish make the asters full.

Finally, I've found a way to lend my dust:
to phlox and pansies splitting apart the toes,
to dahlias and lilacs bursting in the breast,
and out of my head, unpruned, the rose.

Still Life With Life

Fragrance of lemon after all these years
lingers in the little space that Claesz has caught
as though they had been lately called away,
painter and eater, to another room,
berries abandoned, goblet growing warm
in the long afternoon.
        She'd looked at him
in such a fashion as to stir the wine
out of its still life, found the clever hand
more to contend with than a moment's time.

Evening or morning, soon their careless whim
dissolves in a different light,
        and still this bread
tells of a human hunger almost fed
murmuring in the umber beyond the frame.

El Greco: *The Penitent Magdalene*

Here is no solid rock to worship by,
but Magdalene. Her eyes, her hair, her clothes
as sensuous and unsettled as the sky
of light and liquid, while her passion flows
as deeply as before. Here is no dull
penitent, but one redeemed and torn
away from death's obscure and empty skull
to feel the pleasure of her love reborn.
She, with her hands now folded strong and calm
that once anointed his untended feet
with tears of gratitude and precious balm,
has made the shame of our forgiveness sweet,
in flesh that spirit only could discover,
has found at last our best and final lover.

Degas: *The Morning Bath*

The simple light makes shapely all the air,
especially, to her lover's eye, the form
of this abundant woman. In their warm
room, across the crumpled bed they share,
he captures this endearing glimpse of her
entering her bath: the graceful, steady arm,
half-hidden breast, back curved above the firm
peach appealing billow of her derrière.
It was a happy night. A fragrance seems
to fill the room, like summer by the sea.
There's singing as, outdoors, a cheerful maid
hangs linen freshly laundered for the dreams
of nights to come. And momentarily,
the painter lover puts his brush aside.

The Waterfall

In the Chinese painting
a waterfall occurs
in between what is painted.
What is not there is as much there
as what is. So
many things happen
which seem not to happen.
We are aware
of consequences.
Each cell making a tiny sound
as it sucks in
its bit of air.
I am not there although
you hear my presence
at a great distance
like the waterfall
of Xu Daoning.

Barcarolle Chinoise

The dream story on a Chinese scroll
    unfurls in mist and mountain waterfall
the swirling vision of a dragon's tail.

Calligrapher, whose eye delighted here,
    you breathed the energy of ancient air
and brushed the traces of your character

upon this silken lake whereon I row,
    unrolling time, to contemplate the Tao,
a single heron, rain falling, the thunder's echo.

Lipchitz: *Song of the Vowels*

Two bodies, reinvented in this bronze,
embrace. The implications of their parts
balance like a bridge that occupies its arcs
with holding still and moving all at once.

Solid as light and certain to the eye,
forever inconsummate and complete
as angels, these fresh forms articulate
the first creation cast another way,

and from the struggle of these silent shapes
in their desire to wrestle and to fly,
our feathery, unfinished deity
evokes eternal syllables of grace.

Shelter

If I were homeless, I'd live under here,
he said, patting the massive flank
of Henry Moore's *Sheep Piece* lodged
hugely on the gallery lawn. The two bulks
looming together form an arc, a cove
no wind or shock could ever shake.

Around these solid shapes, in an English field,
a flock once gathered, rubbing a lanolin shine
on the shins of the bronze. The hollow where
those great bellies meet holds off the rain
and, shrouded in fog, the sculpture sucks the cold
into its metal marrow. Curled under there,

lamb or boy could spend the night in peace.
Open to the public now this big embrace
waits for the lost, a permanent address
as kind as any for some wandering soul
who looks each evening for a spot to sleep,
a starlit shelter on the artful green.

The Bride's Mirror Speaks

Your clothed body moves
like wine in an Egyptian jar, nudging
all ways at once.
                    Slowly
a cluster of wild mushrooms
emerging from dull leaves.

Maillol would find a reason
for those thighs, but not
in bronze.
                    Your breasts
are nuns with two delicious thoughts
they do not tell each other.

Taut as silk in the wind, your belly
under a man's hand billows
its tender resistance.

You are an apple tree in the rain.

Docent

The art museum behind the big bronze door.
The yellow buses lining up outside.
The little children eager to explore.

The chirpy docent: Who's been here before?
Please pay attention. I will be your guide.
At this museum, behind that big bronze door,

there's nudity, depravity, and gore
to take your little psyches for a ride.
You children will be able to explore

the beauty born of fear, of faith, of war,
of ancient ritual and genocide
that cannot hide behind a brazen door.

Beheadings hardly happen anymore.
Most artists have avoided suicide.
You children are encouraged to explore

the human drama we cannot ignore,
the shape of visions and the forms of pride
collected here behind the big bronze door.

You'll find despair, anxiety, and more.
Your eyes will bleed. Your skulls crack open wide.
Have fun. Enjoy yourselves as you explore
the art museum behind the big bronze door.

Rites of Passage

Touring the Capitol

for Don Hall

Under the dome, the blue Troop pauses to wonder
only how long until lunch. The writing on the wall
about God and the truth ringing the dim rotunda
       impresses them not at all.

The land cries again for a primitive, naked scout
who alone can explain the old code to these shuffling young,
when the bronze images hold their wild mysteries out
       in an unknown tongue.

Eviction

News item, The Kansas City Star

I'm just the guy they send to change the locks.
But what I seen would make your stomach turn.
Dead kittens. Rotten garbage. Baby blocks.
Rooms all charred up with stuff they tried to burn.
One time I even seen a waterfall
come down the stairs, the bathtub falling through
the ceiling. You could say I seen it all.
I wonder what this country's coming to
when people working just as hard as me
get caught up in some paper-shuffle trick
and end up on the street. I get to be
the one that catches shit. It makes me sick.
I got my job to do. The neighbors stare
like I'm the bad guy, like I didn't care.

Handling the Evidence

Returning from lunch at the Myron Green Cafeteria
we of the jury, heavy with overcooked carrots
and homemade gravy, settle into the box
for the afternoon. A denim jacket gets handed
around. I study the shoulders of the accused
that shaped its slouch. Here is the evidence
(his old pants with the plaster dust lodged in the cuffs)
that he did unlawfully enter. This pair
of ravaged sneakers did, I'm sure, unlawfully
enter. I think of the man being crudely stripped
of these clothes. Handling the evidence of his life
as though I were picking up after a child
half in anger, half in love
I pass it on.

At the Home

His head bobs a continual, involuntary
assent. He only remembers
the nights she comes, fragrant
as a melon left in the sun
with her tan skin under her uniform. Then
she listens to his silent wish. She gives
what she will for the old man's sake: nun
of a new order, Daughters of Abishag,
peeled to the flesh she slides
as warm as a lamb, human
into his bed. His body forgets
but his mind says yes,
yes, I am a man. By day
her breasts as she bends
to tuck in the robe on his lap
touch his face. Some say
that he smiles. How well he looks.
The old man looks
very well. And he nods. Yes.
Yes. Yes.

Abishag: 1Kings 1: 1-4

An Old Man Makes Chili for Lunch

Do you have a poem for an old man making chili for lunch?
Like watery eyes from onion crunching—sneezing
from pepper thrown... e-mail from Dad 5/5/05

He shoves the onion pieces in a pile
to one side as he chops and chops some more.
This cutting board has lasted quite a while
through salty tears of choppers gone before,
but no use buying new equipment now.
Sometimes there's comfort in a kitchenette
that holds what downsized spaces will allow
of former habits. He will not forget
those other hands that held this knife and chopped
for slaw and meatloaf, casseroles and stew,
and apple walnut salad. When they stopped,
he stepped up, making chili, making do,
sneezing on pepper, living on his own.
He cooks for one, but never eats alone.

What Did You Do in the War, Daddy?

for W. E. K.

For twenty years, my father bore
the splendid ribbons of a war
upon his daily uniform.
His hands were good; his eyes were warm;
and when we ran to his embrace,
we never searched our father's face
for shadows. He seemed much the same
as any man who went and came
from offices where things were done.
The war he fought in had been won;
and so, each day, he came and went
maintaining the establishment
of peace. We children never knew
how many hundred times he flew,
what flames he dreamed of, cries he heard—
only the kind, paternal word,
the satisfying discipline.
And he fought on, detached, within.

A Note to My Old Age

By now you shall have counted out my fears
on many fingers, and I count them too
because I know I am already you
remembering myself from your old years.

How loved you were: your hands, your heavy breasts,
your laughter, and the secret talk of eyes,
the vivid mouth, the spreading lap of thighs
(beloved woman, warm and fully blessed

whose laughter lined our face with troughs for tears!)
I write this down in order to prepare
a kind of perfume for your sallow hair,
a kiss, a love song for your wrinkled ears.

Rite of Passage

At thirty-five, she wishes to escape
gravity, the way it defines a woman
against her will. Emerging wet and new
from behind the plastic curtain, she
softens in the fogged mirror toward herself
believing faults have become favors
        in the forgiving.

With an inward lightness, she imagines
how love looks on her.
Weighing time by touch, she finds
each breast alert to its kind appraisal,
approves the familiar pockets
that no longer hold mysteries.
As warmth on wax enables shapely change,
so was she eased into self-knowing
through these years accepting
something like a god having his way
        to husband her.

Thinking of lilacs, she lifts her arms
and pulls down blossoms on her head,
smiling for the child she would not be
again. Behind her the reflection
grows clearer. Lightly she comes to herself
again in the comfortable flesh,
        opens the door.

Advice to a Younger Woman

We used to say when we'd been
loved and left again,
I think I'll move to a different town
and start all over as a virgin.

Who knew how possible it was?

We misplaced the truth
and fixed our minds on facts
as women do
who think they can defend
themselves. Thus our war
begins. We drag up the past
and aim it at our own hearts.
We try to set down the future
like a map.
Safe, but hungry
we take refuge inside walls.

My young friend, you flash your eyes
like mirrors signaling distress.

Start over.

Imagine yourself courageous
at the gate of a different town,
prepared to live in that one place always
alone, without weapons, at peace.

You will become
that pure being about whom
the whole universe
revolves.

Fantasy

When woman wanders brazen in her mind,
no vow can hold her and no fetter bind.

Stone, veil or shutter cannot keep her in,
no man discern how faithless she has been

who sleeps with gods behind the hooded eyes,
ecstatic where her faithful body lies.

A Kind of Clothing

Folds, openings, mouths, a kind
of clothing is what
a woman is,
holding, gathering,
covering the intimate
appearances
of others. A man, a child
put on and take off her body
that belongs to them
before she discovers herself
alone.
Even God wanted to
enter into this garment
to be known.

Deliverance

The red stain appearing
reminds me again of the children
never to be born.
Women are taught we are life-bearers
but we are not.
We are the deliverers
of death.

Ask yourself, my husband, who—
who gives the life, who gives up
a little life whenever we find
each other?

Men rush gladly into death, victims
of their own courage. Too much
they prefer their faceless wars
over the terror of translucent,
immediate girls into whom their bodies sink
and sink and sink.

Oh my beloved,
I am grateful for your giving,
so like death.
I bring you at the very least
my peacefulness.

So let's stir up what joy we can
as though we could all by ourselves
make life together.
Something happens between us
that belongs to
neither you nor me, as we are one
electric flesh only
for a moment

before this death intrudes.

I feel you falling
slowly asleep. It takes years.

I lie awake, holding your body
like a realized pietà,
unable to save you who so willingly
enter into the opened earth.

Hippopotamus

All day the hippopotami
deep in the languid waters lie
which sometimes gently stir and seethe
when they lift up their heads to breathe.

Together thus the he and she
restore themselves to energy
until the blood begins to move
with massive pulse of mammoth love.

Then how the waters crash and churn!
Unquenchable the hippos burn
with every passion of their kind
in boundless flesh and fervent mind

till echoing for miles around,
their natural ecstatic sound
inspires an answering refrain
from every creature on the plain.

O love, as languidly we lie
late in our bed, warm thigh to thigh,
and slowly wake, there thrills through us
The Song of Hippopotamus.

Lovers After a Long Time

Somehow we've chosen to spend this afternoon
separate in rooms each
with its cat, the black and the white, and rain
closing the outer doors.
Only the quiet
arcs between us
like the bridge in a Japanese garden
over the pond full of spotted fish, still
and dreaming with their eyes open.

The State of Absolute Nap

Its conditions are rare. You must be free
of all desires but one: to sleep. You must be alone,
completely isolated from the compelling hum
of traffic or tv. There must be no phone,
unfinished book, or business left undone,
no guilt about neglecting anyone,
and nowhere to go too soon.
Let there be rain on a long afternoon
in the deep woods, at the end
of a long path, where no one will come,
after the last word with a listening friend.

Walking on Water

Squaw Creek

for Linda

1.
Even if we could walk on this field of water
the grass would drown us.
Canada geese move like black letters
in loose paragraphs across the sky.
Afloat in formation, all facing
one way, the mallards make small talk.
We watch them arise by the hundreds,
circle, and sit down again on
what's left of the pond in October
after no rain for weeks.

2.
The place where I was when, as a child,
I first saw a redwing blackbird
comes to mind each time I see one.
The same way I remember the first time
I read certain words, like rubicund.
Rubicund reminds me of elephants, of one
elephant in the *National Geographic*, its trunk
rubicund with scrubbing in the Ganges,
and the fascination of that pendulous
trunk, and the sex of the word sprung
from my own innocent wilderness.

3.
My redwing, flashing its epaulets,
first whirred to life from a slough alongside
a northshore highway on Long Island.
I know you, I thought then, claiming

the pleasure like Eve's of naming things for
the first time: Scarlet Tanager. Arachnid.
Cumulonimbus. Orion. Through the swales of Squaw Creek
wind shudders in stanzas across the grass. The clouds
slump low. No shadow drags under the slow wings
of the blue heron.

Getting Ready to Walk on Water

for Gib

"I have cancer," you told me, glancing aside
like a man confessing a sin he couldn't avoid.
"The prospects are good. It's early," you explained.

That day in the long summer of drought, it rained.
Miracles happen. I'll pray up one for you
as good as rain. That God of plagues and laws,

His eye on sparrows, counts each new gray hair
in your beard, too, Whose touch divides the fear
to give us solid ground to walk across,

pursued and harried by the ghosts of loss
from former lifetimes wasted in complaint.
Keep going, and you'll come out like a saint.

In Memoriam

Adele Coryell Hall

The planet measures out impartial rain.
The clouds let down the deluge where they must
upon the city pavement, thirsty plain,
equally on the blessed and the unjust.
And anywhere, by flood, perhaps, or drought,
the firmament may open or withhold
whatever meaning might be thought about
in ancient stories endlessly retold.
Today the rain is ticking on the glass
between my darkened study and the sky,
dropping the hope of springtime in the grass.
In shallow ground where roots and ashes meet,
the black earth quickens underneath my feet.
The traffic hisses as it passes by.

Sisters

Row upon row, as once they sat in choir,
the nuns are resting underneath their stones,
while winter trees embody them like bones
that resurrect their song and send it higher.

Spirit of God, Sophia, sister, mother,
your music of compassion never dies;
in you perfected voices will arise,
each one the antiphon of every other.

New Year's Eve

The clever nest has shaken from the tree
to land here on the sidewalk at my feet,
as winter clears away last year's debris
and sweeps its brown detritus down the street.

So much depends on something letting go,
a loosening of ties, a stripping clean,
a useful emptiness by which I know
of singing birds that I have never seen.

Found on a Slip of Paper in a Crack in the Wall

for Irina Ratushinskaya

In prison I had two books
someone had left there,
in a language I did not understand,
in an alphabet I did not know.

So I passed the time inventing
stories to put sounds in the teeth
of those letters, to make bread
out of all those delicious words.

Then I began to sing them
over and over, sending their sounds
squeaking into the air like mourning doves,
like the humming of wind through fence wire,
like the applause of leaves.

Then I began to dream them,
and every night they sank into darkness,
like old inscriptions going down
in the hold of a small treasure ship
lost on a terrible sea.

At the Gate

The garden says *Bring order*.
The field says *Let me be*.
The clematis likes fences.
The milkweed wanders free.

Around the bedded lilies
the artful pathway goes.
But where the edge of day is
only the prairie knows.

Climbing

I have begun to narrow down desire.
As though tracing a river to its source
I climb, charting the change higher and higher
from placid meander to the turbulent course
where it began. I have loved much, not well,
collecting worlds to carry on my back.
What shall I leave? The spirits that compel
this climb demand a spare and steady pack.
Leave beauty, wonder. They are everywhere.
Leave hope, and drink from the relentless stream.
Leave knowledge, learn trust in the nimble air
until, suspended by a slender dream,
you seek only to climb, and not to know
where you came from, where you have to go.

When I Become Transparent

When I become transparent,
I shall be a glass,
or prism, or a water bead
upon a vein of grass.

When I become transparent,
I shall be the sky,
or a single facet
in an insect's eye.

When I become transparent,
the universe will be
a little less invisible
through my transparency.

About the Author

Barbara Loots is widely published in the world of formal poetry. Her work has appeared in anthologies such *The Helicon Nine Reader, The Muse Strikes Back, The Random House Treasury of Light Verse, The Whirlybird Anthology of Kansas City Poets, The Random House Book of Poetry for Children*, Thomas Locker's picture book, *Snow Towards Evening*, and in textbooks from Houghton-Mifflin. Her poems are included in *Landscapes With Women: Four American Poets.* A vast quantity of her verse and prose was published during her forty-one years as a writer and editor for Hallmark greeting cards, editions, and children's books. *Road Trip* is her first solo poetry collection.

In Kansas City where she lives, Barbara conducts tours as a docent at the renowned Nelson-Atkins Museum of Art. She serves on the board of a national organization in the USA supporting the work of fourteen schools in the Punjab region of Pakistan. She resides with her husband, Bill Dickinson, and a gray tabby in a 1908 house in the historic Hyde Park district.

Made in the USA
Lexington, KY
09 April 2014